THE GOSPEL OF THE KINGDOM IN ROMANS

THE GOSPEL OF THE KINGDOM IN ROMANS

By Henry Hon

(Excerpts from **God's Kind** and **One Truth** by the same author)

ONE
BODY LIFE

www.onebody.life

TABLE OF CONTENTS

PREFACE

The Epistle to the Romans by the Apostle Paul is considered to be a theological masterpiece painting a complete portrait of God's full salvation. Theologians of all denominations have expounded upon this letter perhaps more than on any other portion of the New Testament. Consequently, most students of the Bible may not expect to discover any new doctrine or helpful practice from the study of this letter.

However, this short booklet may deliver an impactful surprise. Readers will find a fresh perspective that has far reaching impact upon the gospel and the Kingdom of God. In fact, after considering Romans as presented in this booklet, you may recognize that this fresh perspective has been hidden in plain sight for nearly 2000 years. While most expositions have focused on the systematic development of chapters 1-8, chapters 9-16 have been expounded in a piecemeal fashion: treating each chapter as individual topics.

This booklet may be unique in its perspective concerning Romans chapters 9-16 as one systematic development of the gospel of peace for the building up of God's Kingdom, which is the Lord's one Body. **The gospel of peace** is needed in bringing believers together into one ekklesia (aka "church"). When diverse believers are one then God is glorified and Satan is crushed.

The **gospel of the Grace of God** through Jesus Christ has been preached to just about every corner of the earth with millions upon millions of individuals having experienced salvation by grace through faith. However, divisions among God's people continue to increase. Therefore, in order to have the "completion of the blessings of the gospel" (Rom. 15:29) this essential aspect of the gospel — **the gospel of peace** — is now needed more than ever. The gospel of the Kingdom consists of both grace for individual salvation and peace for uniting divided believers.

The content of this booklet is taken from two similar chapters in two of my books: *One Truth*, and *God's Kind*. This is made into a stand-alone booklet to provide a concise vision and practical solution in these days of increasing factious behavior and intolerance. I hope this will be helpful to believers of all stripes as it has been so helpful to me and an increasing number who have not only seen but are experiencing these two aspects of the same gospel.

HENRY HON

1.

THE GOSPEL OF PEACE BREAKING DOWN SEPARATING WALLS

The four Gospels, in general, can be considered the gospel of Jesus Christ before His death and resurrection. Romans can be considered as the gospel of Jesus Christ after His resurrection. Many theologians estimate Romans to be Paul's complete theology of the Christian life (aka, "the Romans Road").

The last verse concluding Acts has Paul preaching the Kingdom of God and teaching the things which concern the Lord Jesus Christ (Acts 28:31). The implication is that Paul's letters and the continuation of Acts were focused on the gospel of the Kingdom. His heart was set on furthering the good news of the Kingdom and the things of Jesus Christ. Therefore, Paul's gospel to the saints in Rome (the first epistle after Acts) must reflect what had filled His heart. He would not write this theological treatise without directly addressing the Kingdom and the things of Jesus Christ.

First, let's consider the timeframe when Paul wrote his epistle to Rome. He had not yet been to Rome, nor was there a record of any other apostle having gone to Rome. Nevertheless, from his writing, *"To all who are in Rome, beloved of God, called to be saints"* (Rom. 1:7), it is apparent there was a sizable community of Christians in Rome, as shown in Romans 16.

In Rome, there were groups of believers meeting in different homes who had come to faith in Christ through various preachers. Some of them might have heard the gospel while traveling through Asia Minor. Many Jews would have visited Jerusalem for the feast days where they must have encountered followers of "The Way." These would have brought the gospel back to Rome. Therefore, believers in Rome were as diverse as the population of Rome. There were well-to-do believers with large households and slaves, Jews, Greeks, barbarians, Roman citizens, and freemen throughout the Empire. In such a situation, it certainly would have been easy for the Christian community to segregate and separate themselves from each other. Naturally, those with similar cultural backgrounds, socioeconomic status, ethnic identities, apostolic preferences, and those with a kosher diet preferred to group themselves together. At least five separate groups can be identified in Romans 16.

Paul's main challenge was bringing the Jewish and Gentile believers together in Rome, which is to be expected from the deep-seated divisions and hostilities that existed between them. Even Peter, with other Jewish believers, separated himself from eating and fellowshipping with believers in Jesus from Gentile backgrounds in Antioch (Gal. 2:2-16). Peter became factious and played the role of the hypocrite even after he preached the gospel in Caesarea at the home of Cornelius, a Gentile who was a Centurion soldier of the occupying legions of the Roman Empire. Peter's example illustrates how easy it is for Jewish and Gentile believers in Rome to separate themselves from each other. If Paul could solve this division problem in Rome, then all other divisions between Barbarians and Romans, slaves and freemen, or the myriads of divisions between Christians today would be comparatively simple to solve. The building up of the Lord's Kingdom depended upon breaking down the "wall of separation" (Eph. 2:14). Let's review the book of Romans with the unity of God's Kingdom in view and division being the problem for Paul to resolve.

Paul addressed this letter to the *"saints in Rome"* (Rom. 1:7). He didn't write this letter to any specific group, not even the group of saints meeting as the Lord's ekklesia[1] in Priscilla and Aquila's house (nor is any leadership designated in his epistle to the Roman saints). He wanted all the saints in the various groups to hear the same message directly from him; after reading, they would come together in one fellowship. Although he was addressing "saints" — those who already had faith in Jesus Christ — yet he said he was **preaching the gospel to them** (Rom. 1:15). According to our current understanding, the gospel message is for unbelievers. Why would Paul need to preach the gospel to those who had already believed in Jesus Christ? It's because they were divided; therefore, they needed to hear and understand the entire gospel of God (Rom. 1:1) concerning His Son, Jesus Christ, Who died and was resurrected (Rom. 1:3-4) for His eternal purpose of His Kingdom to be fulfilled.

---

1   The Greek word "ekklesia" has been mistranslated to "church" in English since the King James Version popularized it. Ekklesia was the forum for practicing a democratic government as invented by the Greeks (c. 600 BC). The citizens of a city-state were "called out" to have their democratic legislative assembly (ekklesia), which made decisions for the benefit of their city. On the other hand, the etymology of the word "church" is a physical building for worship, as nearly all English dictionaries define it as a building for worship. This matter of the Lord's ekklesia (translated into "democratic assembly" in this book) versus "church" will be discussed in more detail in the appendix of this book.

Since the challenge was to bring divided and separated believers into the United Kingdom, Paul started by showing no matter the gulf of differences between believers from Jewish or Gentile backgrounds, they still had a common heritage. The first commonality is sin: both God's condemnation of it and the consequences of sin — the *"wrath of God has passed to all humankind for all have sinned and come short of God's glory"* (Rom. 3:23). In Romans chapters 1 through 3 Paul made evident, whether Jews or Gentiles, whether "chosen" with God's law or without law, both were sinners falling short of God's glory — under the sentence of "judgment." The verdict has already been rendered, and now humanity awaits the execution — "for death passed upon all men" (Rom. 5:12). There is no advantage of Jews over Gentiles or vise-versa regarding condemnation — they are both outside of God's Kingdom awaiting God's judgment upon sin.

As people equally condemned under God's wrath, both needed common redemption through the death of Jesus Christ (Rom. 3:24). Without exception, the only common way to justification before God is through faith (Rom. 4-5) the faith of Jesus Christ (Rom. 3:26). In Romans 4, while the Jews considered Abraham to be their forefather, it made clear Abraham is the father of faith for both Jews and Gentiles (for *"righteousness was imputed to him"* before Abraham was circumcised — Rom. 4:22). Justification was not based on the lineage of Abraham but upon the faith of Abraham.

Romans 6:3-4 unveils both Jews and Gentiles have been "put to death" through Christ's crucifixion and burial. Now, both are sanctified (made holy) the same way. . . by their common identity in Christ.

Romans 7 reveals whether a Jew is under the law or a Gentile without law, both have a common struggle with indwelling sin, and both need the indwelling Spirit as found in Romans 8. It is this Spirit who brings both once-divided people into the glory of the sons of God — from death into life.

From a salvation perspective, Romans 8:29-30 ends with glorification — this should be the finality of the gospel. Glorification is the end goal of every believer's salvation journey. Through these eight chapters, one's salvation is made complete: starting with justification through faith; then sanctification through identification in Christ's death and resurrection; then transformation through the indwelling and leading of the Spirit; and finally, glorification or the transfiguration of the body unto becoming mature sons of God (Rom. 8:29) — ultimately, bringing in the new heaven and new earth. These first eight chapters of Romans are the work of the gospel of the grace of God: all are saved by grace (Rom. 3:24), and after entering grace, all need to stand and remain in grace through the entire salvation journey (Rom. 5:2). Yet, this is only half the book of Romans. Why is there a need for another eight chapters (Romans 9-16)?

Although individual salvation is established and completed, God's purpose is still not fulfilled. The Jews and Gentiles are still divided and most likely gathering separately in Rome; therefore, the Kingdom of God was not mentioned; there was no glory to God and no crushing of Satan. All the major items of God's eternal purpose were missing.

Believers Were Divided: Who Is Special and Chosen?

The bulk of Bible commentaries on the book of Romans has been focused on Romans 1-8. These first 8 chapters clearly have a systematic progression. Contrastingly, Romans 9-16 are usually taken piecemeal, with various disjointed doctrines selected within these chapters. Romans 9 is a pillar of support for those holding the doctrine of election and predestination. Those leading individuals to salvation will find verses in Romans 10 indispensable for gospel preaching. Romans 11 is essential for studying the end times concerning Israel in Bible prophecy. The doctrine of the Body of Christ with the priesthood of all believers can be found in Romans 12. Those objecting to the bid to influence and shape secular government will no doubt use Romans 13. Ministers with a socially liberal perspective of live and let live will derive their doctrine from Romans 14 and 15. Romans 16 has no theology other than to exploit a few verses to ostracize troublemakers in a church while showing Paul's familiarity with various saints in Rome.

What if Paul also wrote Romans 9-16 with a systematic development? What would be the logical progression? From the gospel's perspective, Romans 1-8 is the work of the **gospel of the grace of God** (Rom. 1:16; cf. Acts 20:24), turning condemned sinners into glorified sons of God. In Romans 9-16, readers would be shown the work of the **gospel of peace** (Rom. 10:15; cf. Eph. 6:15), turning believers in divided groups into one unified Kingdom, giving glory to God and crushing the head of His enemy — Satan (Rom. 16:20).

> As it is written, "Jacob I have loved, but Esau I have hated." . . . even us whom He called, not of the Jews only, but also of the Gentiles [ethnos or nations]? As He says also in Hosea: "I will call them My people, who were not My people, And her beloved, who was not beloved." "And it shall come to pass in the place where it was said to them, 'You [are] not My people,' There they shall be called sons of the living God."
>
> (Romans 9:13, 24-26)

While the background of one's individual salvation journey starts with sin and condemnation (Romans 1-3), Romans 9 starts with two divided groups: Jacob (representing the Jews) and *Esau* (the rest of "mankind"), the Gentiles. The word *"mankind"* in Acts 15:17 is translated in the *Septuagint* [ancient Greek version of the "Hebrew Scriptures"] as *Edom* (aka "Esau"). Anyone reading Romans 9:13 will consider God unfair: He hated Esau and loved Jacob. Those who identify with Jacob, the chosen people, can no doubt feel honored and even proud. The Jews, considered themselves to be the pure descendants of Jacob, the true Israel (i.e., the totality of Israel), can be justified in their contempt for Esau — *"the rest of mankind,"* in which the Jews have classified all non-Jews as Gentiles. Those identifying themselves with Esau (the rest of mankind or the Gentiles) will feel dejected, humiliated, and rejected. After all, Esau was considered a sexually immoral and unholy person who was rejected and found no chance to repent even when sought with tears (Heb. 12:16-17).

However, just a few verses later, God calls those Gentiles who were no longer His people *"His people,"* and those that are not beloved *"beloved"* (cf. Hosea 1:6-11; 2:1; Rom. 9:25-26). Isn't that wonderful? God has just completely reversed Himself from hating Esau to loving Esau; from rejecting Ephraim to calling her "beloved" — now all mankind (Gentiles) — whom the Jews (Israel — the House of Judah) had considered inferior, even as unclean dogs, now they are the ELECT OF GOD? WOW!

Paul quoted from Hosea 2:23, *"I will call them My people, who were not My people,"* in reference to Esau. However, contextually, Hosea was speaking of the so-called "Lost Ten Tribes of Israel" known as Ephraim, Jezreel, Samaria . . . those *"swallowed up by the nations"* (cf. Hosea 8:7-10). These are the same people called Gentiles in Acts 15, where James alluded to them as Ephraim, the lost ten tribes coming back to rebuild the kingdom or the Tabernacle of David. By applying Hosea's prophecy, Paul lumped two groups of people into one common group called Gentiles: Ephraim (the lost ten tribes) and Esau (the rest of mankind).

Remember, the context found in Paul's remarks primarily deals with the division between Jewish Christians and Gentile (*"ethos"*) Christians with Jewish heritage considered themselves as beloved Israel (even "exclusively Israel") while considering believers from among the nations (aka, Gentiles) as inferior. That was the reason Jewish believers were motivated to compel Gentile believers to be like them — keeping the laws contained in ordinances according to Moses and their traditions (especially circumcision — Acts 15:1). In Romans 9, Paul showed that through the prophetic Scriptures (Rom. 16:26) the Gentiles are also beloved and deemed His people. Therefore, Jewish believers should accept and love them as God loves them. Jewish believers should no longer consider themselves superior to Gentile believers since God has only one people, and those being called out from among the nations are now part of the same people — The Israel of God (Gal. 6:16).

Let's skip Romans 10 for now and jump to Romans 11 for further consideration.

> Just as it is written: "God has given them a spirit of stupor, eyes that they should not see and ears that they should not hear, to this very day."
>
> (Rom. 11:8)

> And if some of the branches were broken off, and you, being a wild olive tree, were grafted in among them, and with them became a partaker of the root and fatness of the olive tree . . . You will say then, "Branches were broken off that I might be grafted in." Well [said]. Because of unbelief they were broken off, and you stand by faith. Do not be haughty, but fear. For if God did not spare the natural branches, He may not spare you either.
>
> (Rom. 11:17, 19-21)

The situation is reversed: Gentile believers feel special and superior by pointing out that according to Scripture, Israel (Judah, the Jews) is both blind and deaf. Moreover, God pruned and cut off Israel, the "natural branches," for their unbelief, and they, the Gentiles, as the wild olive branch, are now grafted into Christ (the root of the green olive tree-Jeremiah 11:16), enjoying all His riches. God has cut off Judah-Israel. He has cut off everything of the natural branches. It is the age of the Gentiles. The Gentiles are now the "chosen ones" — "*Israel* [Judah] *has not obtained what it seeks, but the elect* [those called out from among the nations] *have obtained it*" (Rom. 11:7). In their own eyes, Gentile believers think they can now denigrate all the practices of Jewish believers. Why are they still practicing the Sabbath or keeping the Levitical diet and feast days? Don't they know God has terminated all these ordinances and laws? The "Jewish thing" is over!

Knowing Israel is no longer part of the olive tree (broken off), Gentile believers now consider themselves superior to Jewish believers. Those Gentile believers separating and dividing from Jewish believers can find support with this thought: If God cut them off, we can also cut off the Jews. If anyone practices anything Jewish, let's support God's decision by withdrawing from them; these Jewish believers need to know God has already cut off Israel.

Paul reprimanded the Gentiles: Don't be proud, don't boast. If they do, God can also cut off these Gentiles. If these Gentile believers divide and cut off Jewish believers, God will cut them off from the enjoyment of the riches of Christ. They will no longer be under God's cultivation to receive nourishment and the pleasure of His grace.

Paul's conclusion was neither group was better. Whether one identifies with the Jewish group or with the Gentile group – neither group is special nor superior to the other. Neither group is exclusively the selected nor the chosen ones. God has committed all in disobedience (Rom. 11:32). In fact, it was and still is this superior group identity that is dividing and causing a separation among believers – and it's not just ethnic divisions; it is a multitude of practices and doctrines, as well as individual "styles" which are causing division in the Kingdom.

There is only one Kingdom of God. There should not be sub-groups. If there is a division between these groups of Jews and Gentile believers, then both are disobedient because both are dividing God's Kingdom, His democratic assembly (ekklesia) as in Matthew 16:18. Whichever divided group you consider yourself to be in, whichever group you have identified yourself with, whether Jewish or Gentile (or even sub-groups within these two major groups), and you consider your group superior and separate from the others, know this: God has counted all such divided Christians under disobedience!

When a person recognizes he or she is being disobedient, then God can show mercy. God's mercy is upon those who acknowledge their disobedience in dividing from other believers. Just as for individual salvation wherein there needs to be an acceptance of being a sinner who needs redemption before salvation can proceed (according to Romans 3); even so, now if one is in a divided state where fellowship is withheld from those dissimilar, that person needs to recognize it is disobedience, even rebellion. It is at this point God's mercy is available. God's mercy is shown upon such a repentant person who is ready to be built up in God's Kingdom. Just as sinners need to repent in their individual salvation, a believer who is divided from their brethren needs to repent so they can become one with other diverse believers and enjoy all the riches of Christ within the Kingdom.

The Gospel of Peace

In Romans 10, we find the preaching of the *gospel of peace* is what brings believers together:

> But the righteousness of faith speaks in this way, "Do not say in your heart, 'Who will ascend into heaven?'" (that is, to bring Christ down [from above]) or, "'Who will descend into the abyss?'" (that is, to bring Christ up from the dead). But what does it say? "The word is near you, in your mouth and in your heart" (that is, the word of faith which we preach): that if you confess with your mouth the Lord Jesus and believe in your heart that God has raised Him from the dead, you will be saved. ... And how shall they preach unless they are sent? As it is written: "How beautiful are the feet of those who preach the **gospel of peace**, who bring glad tidings of good things!"
>
> (Rom. 10:6-9, 15)

The **gospel of peace** was needed to break down the wall of enmity and unite those divided groups into one. Sinners need the gospel, but so do divided believers. Sectarian believers need to hear the gospel — the gospel of peace. How beautiful are the feet of those who preach the gospel of peace! This gospel of peace brings believers together who once identified themselves with various divided groups.

This is not *another gospel*, as Paul calls it in Galatians 1:6-7 (*"which is not another"*); no, it is the very *"truth of the gospel"* (Gal. 2:14). The gospel of peace is, in fact, the gospel of Jesus Christ. He is the One who came down from above as God. He died and went into the abyss as the God-man. He was raised from the dead as the life-giving Spirit to be in every believer's heart and mouth. It is with the heart they believe in His resurrection, and with the mouth they confess Jesus is Lord. The same confession which gave sinners initial salvation is the same confession that will save believers from division. Jesus Christ is rich to all who call on His name — regardless of whether one considers himself a Jewish believer or a Gentile believer. Those recognizing they are in a divided state will call out to be saved so they can enjoy the Lord's riches. This gospel of peace needs to be preached to all believers in division.

What caused divisions between Jewish and Gentile (Greek/Roman/ Barbarian) believers? According to this chapter, it was the law of Moses. Jewish believers considered the law was nonetheless needed to establish their own righteousness unto salvation.

Faith to them was not enough to be saved. The law was still needed. They were like those in Galatia who started in faith by the Spirit but went back to perfect themselves by seeking justification through the law using self-effort (Gal. 3:3-5). Paul admonished them and told them they were bewitched. They should not go back to law but continue by faith in Christ and walk by the Spirit. Certainly, whether the law was needed for righteousness "unto salvation" would cause a dispute between Jewish and Gentile believers.

It is tragic whenever something is added to the one faith of Jesus Christ among believers (Eph. 4:5) because any addition to the faith of Jesus Christ to achieve another level of salvation or further sanctification will always cause division among the saints of the Lord.

> For the Scripture says, "Whoever believes on Him will not be put to shame."
>
> (Rom. 10:11)

> "Therefore, thus says the Lord GOD, 'Behold, I am the one who has laid as a foundation in Zion, a stone, a tested stone, a precious cornerstone, of a sure foundation: Whoever believes will not be in haste.'"
>
> (Isa. 28:16b ESV)

In Romans 10:11, Paul quoted from Isaiah 28:16, highlighting that believers shall not be put to shame. Isaiah prophesied Jesus as the foundation stone and a cornerstone in Zion. It was speaking of the building up of the temple on Mount Zion. Zion in Jerusalem is the place of oneness for the 12 tribes (Psa. 133). That was the site for building God's temple, which typifies God's Kingdom. Paul used this verse in the context of the gospel of peace in Romans 10. Those who believe in Him should be joined together by the Cornerstone for the building up of the temple.

Often, believers from opposing perspectives would be ashamed to be seen together. How can there be fellowship in Christ if there is shame or the appearance of dishonor to be with those deemed unholy or doctrinally in error? That was the problem between the Jewish and Gentile believers. They were ashamed to be seen together in fellowship. Remember Peter in Antioch, how he and all the Jewish believers separated themselves from the Gentiles (Gal. 2). However, if believers are saved through the gospel of peace, their shame to be with any other believers would be gone.

Only through Christ as the Cornerstone can believers, who were previously ashamed to be seen together, join in fellowship for God's Kingdom. This is the salvation needed for divided Christians today.

Paul brought them back to the basics, the gospel of Jesus Christ, the simplicity of salvation. It is just Jesus. No matter how long a person has been a Christian or how scripturally learned, it is still just Jesus: Who He is and what

He has done. Can it be simpler than believing in your heart God raised Jesus from the dead and calling out upon His name to be saved? NO!

The gospel of peace, which alone can bring divided believers together, is not something other than Jesus Christ. This peace does not occur through complex doctrines, higher learning, or special practices. Peace occurs between believers when they return to this simplicity — the singleness of Jesus Christ.

Consider what divides Christians today; it is not Jesus Christ. It is Jesus plus something else. A certain kind of doctrine, such as whether one can lose their salvation; a practice, such as whether one speaks in tongues or not; or a form of living, as to whether it is holy enough. Those who have divided themselves from other believers due to Jesus plus something else need to hear the gospel again! The gospel of peace brings believers back to the simplicity of faith in Christ alone. Those who preach the gospel of peace are blessed peacemakers, who are sons of God (Matt. 5:9). Their beautiful feet are for God's move on the earth to build up His one Kingdom by reconciling once divided believers together into one fellowship — the fellowship of Jesus Christ (1 Cor. 1:9).

Focusing on Romans 1-8 Has Caused Many Divisions

If we identify the time of the Reformation beginning with Martin Luther as the initiation of the journey through salvation, then his interpretation of Romans 3, which highlights justification by faith, sparked one of the biggest divisions within the Body of Christ — the division between Protestants and Catholics. Both Protestants and Catholics preach Jesus Christ. Yet both have many other doctrines and practices separating them. In both groups, myriads of genuine believers affirm faith in Jesus Christ and have been regenerated by the Holy Spirit.

Those in each camp may believe God has chosen them and rejected the other camp. Therefore, due to their group identity, a believer who attends a Protestant church may not fellowship or break bread with one who identifies as a Catholic, and vice-versa. Consequently, how can individuals in either one of these camps get saved from division and into the enjoyment of the Kingdom?

This *gospel of peace* is sorely needed. The gospel of Jesus Christ needs to be preached to those divided into Protestant and Catholic camps. Those who hear this gospel will receive faith to realize barriers between believers have broken down. No matter which group they associate with, they can fellowship freely with others not in their group. Hearing the gospel again, the gospel of peace, brings those divided believers back to Jesus Christ and His riches — together with those with the same faith, enjoying the same riches.

Although the gospel can be preached to many people at one time, receiving the gospel is an individual decision. Indeed, the gospel of grace can be preached to hundreds or thousands at a music concert or an event, yet the acceptance is personal. This is also true of the gospel of peace. This gospel can be preached in a denominational church to many Christians all at once, but the revelation and acceptance are also personal. The church, as an organization, cannot receive the gospel. Receiving the gospel of peace is an individual decision.

This gospel of peace is not for bringing together the Protestant and Catholic church organizations. This gospel cannot be received by an organization; it can only be received by individuals. Those who receive the gospel of peace will realize all walls dividing believers are broken down, which extends fellowship to all types of believers without partiality.

In addition to justification by faith, Paul's Epistle to the Romans includes more doctrines that support believers in following Jesus. For example, Paul addresses the subject of sanctification or holiness in Chapters 5-7, and he highlights the matter of the Spirit in Chapter 8. Just as Martin Luther discovered justification by faith in Romans chapters 3, 4, and 5, many ministers have uncovered helpful doctrines over the last few centuries. Each discovery has benefited followers of Jesus.

Those who have received these doctrinal benefits have been revived and energized. Naturally, they chose to join these ministers or churches (or "ministries") who helped them receive a new spiritual understanding or experience. Consequently, groups developed that consisted of those who have arrived at a similar state of spirituality. They consider themselves truly blessed — due to these new and helpful understandings and experiences.

They thank God for their awakening due to these progressive discoveries from Scripture. These consider themselves blessed to have received God's favor and benefitted from such restoration ministries. Unfortunately, this seemingly innocent and natural progression has resulted in believers dividing and segregating from other believers who had yet to arrive at this new understanding or have taken a different approach to following Jesus.

For example, Joe was a typical church-going Christian who was born again when he was younger. He went to church regularly and liked to party with friends. Consequently, Joe's church attendance started to drop. One day someone asked him to listen to a preacher. The preacher spoke about being filled with the Holy Spirit and how to experience the baptism of the Holy Spirit. Joe was intrigued. He went a few more times, then prayed for this experience. A minister prayed for him, and he got filled with joy and started manifesting a gift of the Spirit.

He was so strengthened that he gave up partying with his friends. He joined this new church which helped him because he felt special. He felt he finally found a church God favored. Looking back at the people in his old church, he thought, "They are really missing the mark, they're deficient." Those in his old church thought Joe was deceived. Neither wanted to fellowship with each other anymore.

Another example: Jill came to Jesus in a "Spirit-filled" church. However, after a few years, she started backsliding. She thought she had lost her salvation because people in her church told her that she would live a holy life if she were truly saved. She constantly felt under condemnation. She doubted whether the Lord was still with her.

One day she heard a minister preaching, "Salvation is all of grace and not of works." Additionally, he said, "Nothing can separate her from the love of God." The minister said that she cannot lose her salvation once she is saved. Jill was so relieved! As a result of this teaching, her love for God was renewed. She felt so special because now she knew God loved her so much, no matter her condition. She joined the church because it helped her understand she could never lose her salvation. She thought the people in her old church were wrong for thinking God could change His mind if a believer backslid. As if salvation were based on one's works, not God's unchanging love and grace.

These examples are but a few of the myriad of illustrations wherein believers depart from one church to another and, in so doing, unwittingly cause division with other believers. Now, consider thousands of Bible teachers desire to help Christians with various combinations of doctrines and practices in the Bible. Undoubtedly, many will be helped by such ministers. Suppose an individual gets help through minister "so-and-so" with what is perceived to be his dynamic practice or teaching. In that case, that individual will consider the group that helped him to be specially selected by God. Therefore, naturally, believers identify themselves according to the group or the minister which benefited them. They will often stay in association or fellowship *only* with those in their newly-found group from whence they originally got such great help.

Now, here we are, centuries after the Reformation. Thousands of Bible teachers and millions upon millions of Christians later. Alas! Believers are divided by group identity, and everyone who has received help thinks their church or group is special and "chosen." This may all have happened gradually without any sinister intent.

Therefore, Romans doesn't end in chapter 8 — it purposefully continues with chapters 9-16 in preaching the gospel of peace to bring believers together into one fellowship. After the first eight chapters, believers can still be divided into various groups — each group has seemingly valid reasons to believe they are chosen by God, superior. Yet, as far as God is concerned, each is disobedient because they are divided. It is time to recognize God's mercy is needed for all His rebellious, divided people.

Not to Think More Highly

The gospel of peace, on the one hand, illuminates the believer's disobedience in being divisive and factious; and, on the other hand, gives salvation and supplies with the riches of Christ (Rom. 10:12). This illuminating revelation and supply causes a believer to repent anew which in turn brings God's new mercies (Rom. 11:32). At this point, those who have obtained mercy (Rom. 11:30-32) continue into Romans 12 where these "mercies" issue forth in the one Body of Christ:

> I beseech you therefore, brethren, by the **mercies of God**, that you present your bodies a living sacrifice, holy, acceptable to God, [which is] your reasonable service. And do not be conformed to this world, but be transformed by the renewing of your mind, that you may prove what [is] that good and acceptable and perfect will of God. For I say, through the grace given to me, to everyone who is among you, not to think [of himself] more highly than he ought to think, but to think soberly, as God has dealt to each one a measure of faith. For as we have many members in one body, but all the members do not have the same function, so we, [being] many, are one body in Christ, and individually members of one another.
>
> (Rom. 12:1-5)

Romans 12 begins with the "*mercies of God*," which clearly refers back to the end of Romans 11. When a follower of Jesus hears the gospel of peace and repents of their disobedience, even rebellion, for being divisive, they are now ready to see and experience real Body Life. You are ready to present yourself to the Body of Christ (the Kingdom of God). If you only associate and fellowship with those in a designated group and not with others, you are not yet ready for true Body Life. You cannot present yourself to the Body of Christ.

The Body of Christ is comprised of both Jews and Gentiles; therefore, the Body of Christ does not belong to any one group, no matter how scripturally correct or spiritually advanced they are. The Body Life found in Romans 12 cannot happen within any one divided group of people. It's not that you have to leave a group from where you receive help; however, it is necessary you are not limited to that particular group. Only then will you be ready to present yourself to the entire Body of Christ. Then you are ready to fellowship with all believers, regardless of which group with whom they may or may not identify.

This attitudinal transformation, wherein the believer's identification finds fellowship with the entire Body of Christ through the renewing of the mind, enables one to think differently. This renewed thinking is not to think of oneself more highly than one ought to think. In Romans 9-11, Paul exposed the disobedience of those in divided groups because they thought they were superior or "chosen" compared to others. Through the gospel of peace, they received mercies to have their minds renewed. The renewed mind appreciates all other members in the Body, whether Jews or Greeks, rich or poor, bond or free, etc.

This renewal of the mind can value all believers as individuals beyond group identity. A renewed mind cannot see believers with a label. Rather, it sees every believer as a member of the Body of Christ, and every member is necessary. There are many different and diverse individual members, but only One Body. Generally, every church or group gathers Christians who are similar. A Jewish group will gather Jewish believers in Yeshua, a Chinese church will gather Chinese people, a Pentecostal church will gather those who practice the gifts of the Spirit, etc. However, in Romans 12, believers have been released into the freedom of the Body of Christ. The Body has diversity in function (Rom. 12:4, 6). Yet, these are absolutely one in fellowship.

The context of the word "world" (literally, "age" CSB) to which believers should "not be conformed" (or not to allow the "world to squeeze you into its own mold") is not solely focused on sin and the glamour of the secular world. Rather, here the emphasis is the religious world with divided groups and churches. Most Christian teachers apply this verse to sanctification, which Paul has already thoroughly addressed in Romans 6-8. In these later chapters, Paul addresses divisions within the Kingdom and a superiority complex among Christians. Don't be conformed to that world! The transformation here is being delivered from this divisive world among Christian believers into the freedom of the inclusiveness of the Body of Christ.

The Secular World Is Not the Problem in Causing Division

> Let every soul be subject to the governing authorities. For there is no authority except from God, and the authorities that exist are appointed by God . . . Owe no one anything except to love one another, for he who loves another has fulfilled the law . . . Love does no harm to a neighbor; therefore love [is] the fulfillment of the law.
>
> (Rom. 13:1, 8, 10)

When Paul wrote to the Romans, Nero was the Emperor. Nero's regime was undoubtedly the worst government in history facing the early Church. Nevertheless, the Scriptures urged the saints to be subject to the governing body. Paul didn't ask or suggest believers become political and overthrow or change the government (the author does not suggest Christians neglect their civic duty to vote if they are citizens of a democratic society).

Basically, he said to trust God for those in authority. The problem with division is not due to the government. Human government is not the source of division in the Body of Christ. In fact, when a government persecutes believers, believers who are suffering are driven to drop their factiousness and become one. Due to unity, they become revived, strong, and fruitful.

Paul's point in Romans 13 is, "Let's not get distracted with human government, be it good or bad." If believers have a heart for the oneness of the Body, then love is needed. Love is the fulfillment of the law. In chapters 9 and 10, Paul addressed a controversy concerning keeping the Mosaic law. Well, here is the fulfillment of all the laws: love one another (Rom. 13:8)! Love those who are dissimilar, love those with different doctrinal views, and love those with diverse experiences and perspectives — *"he who loves another has fulfilled the law"* (Rom. 13:8).

2.

THE LORD'S EKKLESIA GLORIFYING GOD AND CRUSHING SATAN

Not Judging but Receiving One Another

Let not him who eats despise him who does not eat, and let not him who does not eat judge him who eats; for God has received him . . . One person esteems [one] day above another; another esteems every day [alike]. Let each be fully convinced in his own mind.

(Rom. 14:3, 5)

". . . that you may with one mind [and] one mouth glorify the God and Father of our Lord Jesus Christ. Therefore receive one another, just as Christ also received us, to the glory of God."

(Rom. 15:6-7)

By Romans 14, being in One Body and loving one another is no longer a theory — it has become pragmatic. Jewish and Gentile saints are now assembling together for meals and fellowship. Instead of meeting in separate, divided groups, they come together as the Lord's democratic assembly (ekklesia). According to 1 Corinthians 11, when the Lord's ekklesia assembles, there must (it is necessary) be diversity among believers from various factions. Yes, factions — but not "factious." They could come together for meals, break bread to remember the Lord and fellowship around Jesus Christ.

In Romans 14, some ate meat (presumably unclean), and some ate only vegetables. Some treated one day special (likely, the Sabbath), and others treated every day the same (Rom. 14:5). Previously, in Romans 9-11, these saints might find it much easier to gather separately: Those who would not eat meat would have their own meals and fellowship separately from those who enjoyed eating all kinds of meat. Those who considered one day special would treat those meeting on any day of the week as inferior. Therefore, many of these saints might have gathered exclusively with those who were similar and divided from those who were different regarding how they gathered, worshipped, and fellowshipped on certain days. It's more "comfortable" to gather within your "comfort zone." Frankly, it's much easier to be (however unintentionally) factious.

In practicing the Kingdom, they assembled at the same place and time. In such a situation, love is needed not to judge but to receive one another. It can be awkward initially with the propensity to judge those dissimilar from you. Thus, from Romans 14 to the beginning of Romans 15, the focus is on receiving one another in fellowship, although perspectives and understanding might be conflicting and contrary. In such a diverse environment, love and unity can manifest.

Though diverse, they became one mind and one mouth to glorify God. It does not mean they all agreed to eat meat or keep the same day. *Unity is not uniformity or conformity*; it simply meant their minds were now focused on God's Kingdom, not their differences. The gospel of peace made them one to glorify God. Notably, there was no mention of God receiving glory in Romans 1-8. **It is not until believers are one that they can glorify God**.

Christians speak much about glorifying God. They may specifically focus on holiness to give glory to God, yet up through the believer's own glorification in Romans 8, there was no mention of God being glorified or receiving glory. However, in Romans 15, God is glorified in His built-up *democratic assembly*! Therefore, the following verse charged believers again to receive one another as Christ received each of them. Jesus Christ received each of them in their diverse state through His blood on the cross. Through the same blood of the cross, He brought peace between those who were in conflict . . . bringing both of them into One New Man — into a Perfect Man (cf. Eph. 2:15; 4:13). It is here that God receives the glory from the manifested Kingdom of God.

The Kingdom of God Manifested

". . . for the kingdom of God is not eating and drinking, but righteousness and peace and joy in the Holy Spirit. For he who serves Christ in these things [is] acceptable to God and approved by men. Therefore let us pursue the things [which make] for peace and the things by which one may edify another."

(Rom. 14:17-19)

Paul was a preacher of the Kingdom of God 'till the very end of Acts (Acts 28:31). Clearly, he was absolute for the Kingdom of God. Here, in his complete theological work on the Christian life, the Kingdom of God is revealed. The

Kingdom of God is where previously divided believers are united in the Lord's ekklesia. This is indeed significant! In Romans, the Kingdom of God is not domiciled in casting out demons or in the context of influencing the secular marketplaces of society; rather, it is amid diverse believers receiving, loving, and fellowshipping with one another in one accord.

The Kingdom of God is not related to outward practice — whether one eats, drinks, keeps days, dresses a certain way, or keeps certain laws. It is "righteousness and peace and joy in the Holy Spirit." Righteousness refers to justification by the blood of the Lamb; peace is between once divided peoples; and joy is the experience or manifestation by all those in such a harmonious environment (Acts 2:46). Every time believers assemble in oneness with those who might naturally be contrary to them — this is the Kingdom of God being manifested. Therefore, pursue peace and build up one another!

> But why do you judge your brother? Or why do you show contempt for your brother? For we shall all stand before the judgment seat of Christ.
>
> (Rom. 14:10)

It is also significant in this chapter where relationships between believers may conflict with each other — herein is the judgment seat of Christ revealed. The fact there is judging and contempt between believers assembled means there were divergent views and practices, which is an environment ripe for such negative behaviors. Whoever gives in to their natural reaction and remains in that state of contempt would be liable to be harshly judged by Christ at His coming. This is serious!

According to the context of this verse, to be approved under Christ's judgment, believers must receive, fellowship, love and build up one another. This is not referring to a group of like-minded and similar Christians; rather, it refers to those dissimilar and diverse from each other.

A Differing Measure of Faith

> The faith that you have, keep between yourself and God. Blessed is the one who has no reason to pass judgment on himself for what he approves. But whoever has doubts is condemned if he eats, because the eating is not from faith. For whatever does not proceed from faith is sin.
>
> (Rom. 14:22-23 ESV)

In Romans 12:3, it is clearly written that each believer has a different measure of faith. Some have more faith, and others less. Yet, as long as they have faith in

Jesus Christ, every believer is in the Kingdom. Expecting all believers to have the same measure of faith is an error that will cause judging and separation from one another. There can only be peace and loving one another if there is the acceptance that each believer is different and at various stages of faith.

In Romans 14, the issue is related to eating meat offered to idols or not. On this subject, Paul has enough faith to eat food previously offered to idols because his faith relegated idols to be nothing (1 Cor. 8:4). However, those with weaker faith and knowledge can stumble by offending their conscience if they eat such food.

From a holiness and social acceptance point of view, eating food offered to idols would have been highly controversial and divisive in those days. Perhaps it was more contentious than whether believers today should drink alcoholic beverages, how to dress according to a Biblical code of holiness, and various differing views relating to social issues. There must be allowances made for each believer as to the measure of faith they have to live the way they live.

At the end of Romans 14, Paul said that whatever conviction one may have based on his or her faith, they should keep it between themselves and God. There will be controversial topics and holiness issues that can be divisive when believers from diverse perspectives assemble. Paul said to let the liberty that one has not to cause a stumbling block to others. The goal of a democratic assembly is to remember the Lord and not flaunt liberty or promote a controversial agenda.

Don't push someone to act beyond their measure of faith. This should include either doing a certain thing or not doing it. Returning to the subject of eating food offered to idols: one side can force a believer to eat beyond their faith, while the other can condemn those who eat as being unholy and idol worshipers. The bottom line: all believers should respect each other's measure of faith since anything not proceeding from faith is a sin.

One of the goals of ministry (the five-fold) is to strengthen believers' faith and knowledge so that they may live out fully the life of Christ in them. That should be ongoing as part of equipping the saints (Eph. 4:12). However, when it comes to receiving and fellowshipping in the Lord's democratic assembly, all requirements must be set aside for the sake of the Kingdom of God.

The Completion Gospel

> But I know that when I come to you, I shall come in the **fullness [or "completion"] of the blessing of the gospel of Christ** . . . Now I beg you, brethren, through the Lord Jesus Christ, and through the

> love of the Spirit, that you strive together with me in prayers to God
> for me . . . Now the God of peace [be] with you all. Amen.
>
> (Rom. 15:29-30, 33)

Nearing the end of his epistle, Paul used this phrase: *the fullness or completion of the blessing of the gospel of Jesus Christ*. Remember, the entire book of Romans is Paul preaching the gospel of Jesus Christ to the saints there. He preached being saved by the gospel of the grace of God in Romans 1-8, and now, the gospel of peace wherein believers are brought into unity — into the expression of the Kingdom of God (Romans 9-16). It is at this point the gospel of Jesus Christ has come to its fullness . . . the completion of the gospel of Jesus Christ. Romans 1-8 is the first part of the gospel of Jesus Christ — Romans 9-16 is the completion of the blessing of the gospel of Jesus Christ!

Without preaching the gospel of peace, the gospel of Jesus Christ is incomplete. It is far past time for ministers and preachers to rise up to preach the *Completion Gospel*: both grace and peace. This is the gospel of the Kingdom of God! To highlight and punctuate the gospel of peace as the operating subject of these chapters, Paul ends this section of his writing with: "The God of peace be with all the saints, amen" (Rom. 15:33).

But wait, Satan still needs to be crushed!

Proactively Greet to Initiate this One Fellowship

> Likewise, [greet] the church [ekklesia] that is in their house. Greet
> my beloved Epaenetus, who is the first fruits of Achaia to Christ .
> . . Greet Asyncritus, Phlegon, Hermas, Patrobas, Hermes, and the
> brethren who are with them. Greet Philologus and Julia, Nereus
> and his sister, and Olympas, and all the saints who are with them.
>
> (Rom. 16:5, 14-15)

Those assembling in the manner of Romans 14 and 15 would be considered the Lord's ekklesia (democratic assembly) according to 1 Corinthians 11-14. The Lord's ekklesia is where diverse believers assemble for meals, each with the freedom to speak forth their perspectives of Christ and enjoy the oneness of fellowship in God's Kingdom. In Rome, the ekklesia gathered at Priscilla and Aquila's house (i.e., "the ekklesia that is in their house" — Rom. 16:3-5). Apparently, other individuals would not be included in this ekklesia; also, many other believers were gathering in other separated groups based on the description in Romans 16.

There were the two households of Aristobulus and Narcissus. More than likely, they were notable names of the elites or upper class in Rome (Rom. 16:10-11).[2] A rich household at the time could easily have dozens of people attached and be self-sufficient as a Christian community without having to fellowship with outsiders. Then two other groups were mentioned: a group of names and the "brethren who are with them" and another group of names and the "saints who are with them." From the names and how Paul addressed them, it can be surmised that one was a Jewish group and the other Gentiles. In Romans 9:3, Paul called those Jewish like himself "brethren" and called all in Rome, including the Gentiles, "saints" in Romans 1:7.

With believers already divided between the rich and poor, Jews and Gentiles, Paul commanded the saints in Rome to proactively and intentionally go out of their way to greet one another. They needed to leave the comfort of their natural surroundings with those who were like themselves. They needed to get out and greet those with whom they were unfamiliar.

Just about all teachers of the Bible have considered Romans 16 to be Paul's own salutation/benediction or greeting of various saints in Rome. It is understood to be: Greet so-and-so for me (as in "say hello, or hi, from me, Paul"). As such, the application of this portion is relegated to trying to remember all the saints if you are going to write a letter and don't leave anyone out! However, upon further consideration, it may also be considered that Paul was not sending personal greetings. Rather, Paul was commanding the saints in Rome to go and greet all these various people listed in that chapter. They were to go and greet numerous believers who were segregated from one another. In fact, he used the imperative in Greek to command them to do this greeting seventeen times — it was not "optional" — it was "mandatory" — an injunction!

The word "greet" is not just saying "hi" when walking past someone. The word for "greet" in Greek means: "to embrace, to be joined, a union, to visit or joyfully welcome a person" (*Strong's Dictionary* and *Thayer's Lexicon*). It was customary for greetings to take place by entering a house with the occupant welcoming that person to stay for a while (Matt. 10:12; Acts 21:7). Greetings included intimate dialogues with another person (Luke 1:40-55; Acts 21:19). Additionally, the Greek verb form for "greet" as found in Romans 16 is *aorist middle deponent imperative*; which means Paul was commanding whoever was reading his letter to take continual action to go and greet those listed. This greeting is the initiation of fellowship. They needed to continue doing this greeting whether they had done so in the past or not. Likewise, it isn't a matter

---

of just "meeting" someone, as in: "Hi, how are you doing?" No, no, no — it's a matter of not only seeing but "greeting" — getting to know them!

It is consistent through all the epistles wherein the verb form for "greet" is different whether the greeting is done by someone remotely in another locality or done face to face in the same locality. For example, in Romans 16:16: "Greet one another with a holy kiss. The assemblies [ekklesia] of Christ greet you." In this verse, there are two "greets." The first one obviously is in-person, a face-to-face greeting. The second "greet" is from all the assemblies. Obviously, the saints in those assemblies were not in Rome. Therefore, the verb form is different. Specifically, it was not imperative, a command; rather, it was indicative, a simple statement of fact. Over 37 times, greetings were used in all the epistles. In every single instance, when it was face-to-face, it was imperative, a command; however, when it was remote, it was indicative. Without a doubt, all the greetings in Romans 16:3-15 were Paul commanding the recipients of his letter, which were all the saints in Rome, to greet the saints in those verses. It was not Paul doing the greeting from afar. He was commanding, charging the saints to intentionally, proactively, and continually go and greet all the various saints in Rome.

They needed to do it in person, face to face, and intimately with a kiss. Why is that important? It is important because every believer's situation and relationship with one another in Rome was the closest example of what it is today. Presently, there are a variety of factions and groupings of various believers. These various groupings are generally a result of comfort and familiarity due to similarities in ethnicity, doctrine, worship tradition, etc. Additionally, none of the first-century apostles founded any of the groups we have today. Today, the one fellowship of Jesus Christ is fractured, and the practice of true oneness is severely limited.

Therefore, today the Gospel of Peace in Romans is needed, and specifically, the last chapter with the command to go greet is as critical now as it was 2,000 years ago in Rome. Believers today are to obey the Scriptures just as those in the First Century. God's people should take similar action to go and greet brothers and sisters individually, as well as those associated with other groups. They should do this regardless of whether they have done so in the past.

Members of a home group from the same "church" might enjoy a homogenous fellowship because they're going to the same church — but that's not, per se, an ekklesia. An ekklesia occurs when brethren from diverse groups of believers come together to "meet and greet" one another and meet with very diverse believers who have various doctrines and practices but find their oneness of fellowship in Christ alone!

Therefore, the greeting was not Paul's casual addendum to his otherwise intensely theological discourse. No, it was Paul's way of engineering a mixing of normally segregated people and expanding the fellowship and oneness among all the saints in Rome. If they did not proactively go and greet other believers who were normally not associated with their grouping, segregation and division would persist, eventually becoming systematized and institutionalized after some time.

Enjoining those who would obey Paul's injunction to go and greet all these followers of Jesus in Rome, whether Jews or Gentiles, slave or free, would initiate fellowship among all the Lord's followers in Rome. Such vibrant fellowship is the reality of the one ekklesia. This is what is upon the Lord's heart.

Without this ongoing greeting in Romans 16, Paul's theology concerning salvation, justification, sanctification, and glorification resulting in the Kingdom of God, would be utterly deficient. Without purposeful outreach to have vibrant fellowship with all those of the same faith but not in the same grouping, the saints would succumb to gravitational separation, finding themselves with their "own kind" — whether ethnically, doctrinally, politically, socio-economically, or personality-wise. The result: division and sectarianism.

Therefore, every believer can start preaching the gospel of peace by simply going and greeting those believers unfamiliar or even contrary — fellowshipping with them concerning the person and work of Jesus Christ. This act of extending oneself to greet others in Christ is by itself preaching the gospel of peace. Many Christians consider that preaching needs a sizable audience. No. Just as preaching the gospel of grace is effective on a personal basis, preaching the gospel of peace is as simple and personable as visiting and greeting another believer in the environment of any given neighborhood, workplace, or school.

Greeting Exposes Selfish Ministers

I appeal to you, brothers, to watch out for those who cause divisions and create obstacles contrary to the doctrine that you have been taught; avoid them. For such persons do not serve our Lord Christ, but their own appetites, and by smooth talk and flattery they deceive the hearts of the naive.

(Rom. 16:17–18, ESV)

These verses warning us about division are immediately after the charge to go "greet." This context provides evidence that these commands to greet were specifically written for the oneness of the Kingdom. Sadly, these verses have mostly been taken out of their context and used to abuse believers in churches or Christian groups who are "troublemakers." Typically, those who are contrary or have conflicting ideas with the church they are attending, especially if they start voicing their objections, will be told they are causing a division. Therefore, if they do not refrain from criticizing the church or leadership, these verses will be cited for disciplinary actions.

Not only so, but if these "divisive" members depart from that church or group, often, the rest of the members will be told to avoid them for being rebellious and divisive. The threat of being ostracized from a community of believers helps maintain order within a church. Using these verses in such a way is appalling and wrong.

Now let's consider these verses in context. Paul wanted believers to visit and greet all believers in the One Body in Rome. He warned they would run into believers who decided to stand apart from the common fellowship of God's Kingdom, who would not receive or give such greetings. Christian teachers taught things contrary to the Apostle's teaching of Jesus Christ and His one Kingdom, intending to cause a faction — a standing apart — between those under their teachings and the rest of the believers in Rome. While greetings among all believers were going on, these divisive teachers deceived the hearts of the naïve to corral them into sectarian groups they controlled. They are the "wolves" who "draw away the disciples after themselves" (Acts 20:30).

Today they might say their group is different because they have the "real baptism," and other believers are not baptized properly. Another might say they have a special and higher revelation, so their group is not like other believers because they receive their teachings from minister so-and-so.

Paul appealed to believers to watch out for such teachers and avoid them. This should not be extended to the naïve or simple believers who are deceived by these teachers and their smooth talk; it is not their fault they were misled into a sectarian group. Those who teach differently intending to recruit followers are not serving the Lord. These are serving their own appetite for either material gain or power to control those they have corralled into their sect. This serious matter can only be exposed through indiscriminate greetings among believers. If greetings do not occur between believers in these segregated groups, the self-serving teachers and their groups can stay hidden. But once greetings transpire from house to house, those "standing apart" will be exposed; teachers and leaders of these stand-apart groups should be noted and avoided.

This division in Romans 16:17–18 is much more serious than the "division" identified in 1 Corinthians 1:10. The division there is "schism," a rent or a discord. The "division" in Romans 16 is a much stronger word for dividing and separating. Schism is like a division instigated by a family quarrel which is never good. Sometimes it results in devastating rifts; however, family members still acknowledge they are in the same family, despite the rift. They just need to grow out of such childish arguments. However, the "division" in Romans 16:17-18 is "*dichostasia*," which means "a standing apart" (Vine's). It is like saying: "I am not part of that family. We are our own family." This type of division is deliberate separation, and those promoting such separations must be marked and avoided.

While many ministers today have a pure motive to serve God alone for His Kingdom and not their own "belly," there are other ministers whose motives are to draw people to themselves. By putting Romans 16 into practice, when believers get out of their "comfort zone" and greet all kinds of other believers, the true ministers of God will shine forth for the building up of His Kingdom. Moreover, those intentionally dividing believers will be recognized for their delimiting purposes contrary to building up of God's Kingdom. Forbidding to allow members of your ministry/church to "meet and greet" other brethren outside your immediate group is antithetical to the United Kingdom of God — it is divisive and factious.

Those serving the Lord Jesus Christ for His purpose should teach those under their leadership to follow Paul's command to go, visit, and greet all believers around them, even though they are not in their church or ministry. Those who serve their own appetite to build their own sect do their best to isolate those under their leadership; they do not want their members to be open to greeting and receiving others or be intimate with believers not part of their group.

While selfish ministers are exposed for what they are, the proper ministers of the gospel of Jesus Christ will find themselves more useful, and their function will extend beyond their immediate church confines. Those ministers with a heart for the one democratic assembly will thrive in their ministry to all the saints.

A couple of final observations are in order. Paul's charge to go greet applies to individuals. It was not a charge to go greet any organization. Organizations are impersonal. Churches and ministries as organizations are not living beings. Fellowship is not possible at an organizational level. Therefore, greetings can only be directed to individuals.

For example, it is impossible to greet the Roman Catholic Church or the Baptist Church, but you can greet a believer who is a member of the Catholic Church. You can even greet a pastor of a Baptist Church. You can also greet the minister who has an organized ministry. This greeting has nothing to do with the so-called ecumenical movement, which aims to unify Christian churches and organizations. Romans 16 involves individual believers obeying the Lord to go and greet other individual believers because they are in the same ekklesia, which is God's Kingdom.

Reading through that list of people in Romans 16, in many cases, Paul attached something of interest to a person's name, such as: Greet my beloved Epaenetus, who is the first fruit of Achaia (v. 5); Greet Mary, who labored much for us (v. 6); Greet the beloved Persis, who labored much in the Lord (v. 12). It could be Paul's way to entice believers to go greet them and find out more about their story. The fact is, every believer has an interesting story. Each one is a testimony of how God has changed or used them. Let's go and find out all the marvelous ways He has worked in each of His people — you will not know unless you go and greet them.

Crushing Satan Is a Fitting Finale

> The **God of peace** will soon crush Satan under your feet. The grace of our Lord Jesus Christ be with you.
>
> (Rom. 16:20, ESV)

This declaration of crushing Satan didn't appear in Romans 8 or even Romans 15. It wasn't until the last chapter of the epistle that we read anything about Satan, the Devil, the Serpent, or the Dragon. Satan being crushed at the end of Romans is an answer to the Lord's promise in Matthew 16:18 — "The gates of Hades" would not prevail against His ekklesia. His democratic assembly would crush the gates of Hades, the stronghold and power of Satan. This shows all 16 chapters of Romans are needed by the saints in Rome to crush Satan under their feet. How? Through the GOSPEL OF THE KINGDOM which includes the Gospel of Peace — THE GOD OF PEACE!

The crushing of Satan is the result and evidence that the Kingdom of God is built. God's kind (His children) have matured into one to defeat God's enemy as originally purposed by God.

If Romans was a movie, then many readers of Romans would consider chapter 16 with many names as "rolling the credits of the movie" since Romans 15 already ended with what appears as a benediction and a hearty "amen" in Romans 15:33 (i.e., *Now the God of peace be with you all. Amen.*). Just as many people start walking out of a movie when the credits start rolling, many Bible readers would do the same and not pay attention to Romans 16. However, if this last chapter is skipped, the final demise of the villain being crushed by the heroine would be missed. This shows us that Romans 16 is the climax of the movie. This should not be easily dismissed.

In Paul's presentation of his complete theological framework, we must recognize the entire letter to the saints in Rome was divinely inspired. Each chapter was exactly where it needed to be, with its content precisely expressed. Proclaiming Satan being crushed at the end of Romans 16 shows Satan cannot be crushed by the God of Peace under the saints' feet until the practice of greeting is accomplished. Only then is the Lord's Kingdom (i.e., ekklesia) built up. Yes, it seems odd to state it is THE GOD OF PEACE Who crushes Satan under the feet of the ekklesia — however, this is the result of the Gospel of Peace building up God's Kingdom!

Just think — the same beautiful "feet" who preach the gospel of peace (Rom. 10:15), those same "feet" carrying the saints to go greet, are the same feet crushing Satan. We cannot dismiss the *protoevangelium* ("first gospel") found in Genesis 3:15, where the LORD God said to the serpent: "And I will put enmity between you [i.e., Satan] and the woman, and between your seed and her Seed [i.e., the Messiah]; He [the Messiah] shall bruise your [i.e., Satan's] head, and you [i.e., Satan, the Serpent] shall bruise His [Messiah's] heel [alluding to Messiah's crucifixion]." In fact, the one Seed became a corporate seed. The seed is now the diversity of God's people in oneness: There is neither Jew nor Greek, there is neither slave nor free, there is neither male nor female; for you are all one in Christ Jesus . . . then you are Abraham's seed. (Gal. 3:28-29).

Remember the difficulties for Jews and Gentiles even to eat together? What a beautiful sight of fellowship and oneness when the city of Rome witnessed Jews entering Gentile homes to greet them, having a meal together, and vice-versa. The rich or freemen would greet believing slaves by welcoming them into their homes for a meal. Throughout the city, unlikely people would be greeting and fellowshipping together at markets, "coffee shops," and in their homes, from house to house.

As the number of believers in Rome who read Paul's letter increased, the greetings, and thus the fellowship among the saints, exponentially grew. What a testimony to the oneness of believers as they went from house to house greeting each other! Paul ended this section of his epistle to the saints in Rome by instructing his readers to greet one another with a holy kiss. This kind of greeting expressed pure love and intimate fellowship among believers. None would be isolated in their own group, seeing the same believers year after year, but instead would be part of a growing network of homes in one fellowship with much traffic and support between them because they were indeed one Kingdom.

Today, most believers are segregated and isolated in their church or home. If believers accepted Paul's directive to seek out other believers and "meet and greet" them, the Lord would have a way to unify His Kingdom. There are many churches, ministries, and Christian groups today with believers isolated from each other. It is essential in God's purpose for believers to heed Paul's command to go and greet fellow believers who are not in their own grouping.

In God's eyes, all His children — God's kind — are in one family, the Household of Faith (cf. Gal. 6:10). As such, believers should not acknowledge any division, no matter what church or denomination may segregate Christians. Greetings to believers who meet in the Catholic Church should have the same zeal and love in their greetings given to believers who may identify with a Baptist Church, a Pentecostal Church, a non-denominational church, or even a believer not attending any church at all (so-called "*dones*"). For mutual greetings among believers, no recognition should be given to which church a person belongs (since churches are artificially organized by men).

No matter which church one belongs to or if a believer finds fellowship outside of the institutional church, God wants everyone to proactively greet and receive other believers. What if believers emphasizing Pentecostal experiences greet those who disparage the gifts, like speaking in tongues? What would happen if those who preferred Reformed theology greeted those who preach salvation is a choice? Believers would automatically become one in the reality of the Kingdom of God, and non-essential doctrines which do not "save" in the first place, as well as pet practices, would fade in priority — these peripherals would cease being an issue between believers. Subsequently, intimate fellowship in Jesus Christ alone would cause the ekklesia to bloom from house to house. This would be able to take place outside of and despite almost 2,000 years of separation within institutional Christianity.

How can believers testify to the God of Peace if they are divided? By the God of Peace working among them in action and being magnified among all these greetings of disparate believers. Therefore, Satan being crushed is an appropriate ending for this epistle, but not before. In Matthew 16:18, Jesus was giving a promise or a prophecy. Here, however, Paul and early believers were living out the reality of the practical building up of the ekklesia, the Kingdom of God, which crushes Satan. When believers are in oneness, in this one fellowship, built on this one foundation — Jesus Christ, with all her members functioning and active — then Satan is crushed! The oneness of believers defeats the enemy and satisfies the Lord's desire in His prayer found in John 17: The prayer for His people to be one as the Father and the Son are one.

The Conclusion of Paul's Gospel

> Now to Him who is able to establish you according to my gospel and the preaching of Jesus Christ, according to the **revelation of the mystery** kept secret since the world began.
>
> (Rom. 16:25)

> This is a great mystery, but I speak concerning Christ and the
> church [ekklesia].
>
> (Eph. 5:32)

Paul declared at the end of this epistle: It is his gospel, the preaching of Jesus Christ. He ended it the same way he started . . . separated to the gospel of God, to preach the gospel to the Romans. This proves Romans as the entire gospel of God needs to be preached. Don't preach a half gospel. Preach the Gospel of Grace but don't neglect to preach the Gospel of Peace. By preaching both you will preach the **Completion Gospel** (Rom. 15:29). **This is the Gospel of the Kingdom**. Such preaching reveals the mystery that was kept secret since the world began.

The gospel is not just to save sinners, so they may go to heaven but to complete the mystery of God. What is this mystery the gospel would unveil? In Colossians 2:2, we find the "mystery of God" is Christ: ". . . *that they may know the mystery of God, even Christ*" (ASV). Then, we find in Ephesians 3:4-6 Paul speaks of the "*mystery of Christ,*" which is His Body: "*You can perceive my understanding in the mystery of Christ . . . that the Gentiles are fellow-heirs, fellow-members of the body, and fellow-partakers of the promise* (ASV). Taken together, Paul declares in Ephesians 5:32 the **great mystery** is Christ and His ekklesia!

Ephesians 1:23 says: the ekklesia (democratic assembly), the Lord's body, is the "fullness" or "completion" of the One who fills all in all. It is mysterious and awesome that God's plan is His ekklesia, His people in oneness, who become God's completion or fullness. This word "completion" (*plērōma*) is the same Greek word as the "completion" of the gospel of Jesus Christ (Rom. 15:29). It is the completion gospel: both the gospel of God's grace and the gospel of peace, which will usher in the built-up ekklesia being the "completion" of God. Truly this has been a hidden mystery, but now revealed through Paul's "*completion of the blessing of the gospel of Jesus Christ.*" Let's start preaching this COMPLETION GOSPEL, which is the GOSPEL OF THE KINGDOM, to hasten the end of this age.

> "And this gospel of the kingdom will be preached in all the world as
> a witness to all the nations, and then the end will come."
>
> (Mat 24:14)

> "That they all may be one, as You, Father, are in Me, and I in You;
> that they also may be one in Us, **that the world may believe that
> you sent me.**"
>
> (John 17:21).

Appendix
EKKLESIA VERSUS CHURCH/MINISTRY

A Stone for the Ekklesia Is a Person in God's Kingdom

"And I tell you, you are Peter, and on this rock, I will build my church [ekklesia], and the gates of hell shall not prevail against it. I will give you the keys of the kingdom of heaven, and whatever you bind on earth shall be bound in heaven, and whatever you loose on earth shall be loosed in heaven." . . . From that time Jesus began to show his disciples that he must go to Jerusalem and suffer many things from the elders and chief priests and scribes, and be killed, and on the third day be raised.

(Matt. 16:18-19, 21 ESV)

"You yourselves like living stones are being built up as a spiritual house.
(1 Peter 2:5a)

When Simon (aka Peter) received the revelation that Jesus is the Christ, the Son of the living God, Jesus immediately changed His name from Simon to Peter, which in Greek means a *stone*. As a stone, Peter was material used by the Lord to build His ekklesia. He became a stone to be built on the Rock, who is Christ, the Son of God. That revelation alone qualifies believers to be a stone, a member of the Lord's democratic assembly.

The group of people whom God regenerated to be His Kingdom through the death and resurrection of Christ is called the Lord's ekklesia in Matthew 16. The people who make up the Lord's ekklesia are the same people who are the constituents of the Kingdom of God. They are not two different sets of believers but one and the same. This is a critical understanding: The same group of people belong to both.

The Greek word "ekklesia" has been mistranslated to "church" from the time of the translation of the Authorized Version. The word "church" is literally defined as a physical building for worship; however, ekklesia is a democratic assembly, which will be discussed later in this chapter. For the sake of accuracy, the word "ekklesia" (democratic assembly) will be used to distinguish it from "church" being a physical building or the Christian organizations which own the buildings.

Later, when Peter wrote his epistles, Peter made it exceedingly clear that all regenerated believers are also living stones for God's building. Peter was not the only stone. In chapter 1, he said that all those who have believed in Jesus are born again (1 Pet. 1:20-23). Additionally, their regeneration was due to the resurrection of Jesus Christ (1 Pet. 1:3). Then, in chapter 2, Peter said that even a newborn babe in Christ is a living stone for God's building (1 Pet. 2:2, 5). All believers, as living stones, are material for the spiritual house, which is God's ekklesia (1 Tim. 3:15).

Jesus made it clear that a stone for the building up of His ekklesia has the key or access to the Kingdom of God. That means the entrance into the ekklesia is the same entrance into the Kingdom of God. Peter, in His epistles, made the same connection.

Ekklesia: A Democratic Legislative Assembly

Since the building up of the Lord's ekklesia is the key to the Kingdom of God, it is imperative to have an understanding of His ekklesia. If not, then there can be much study and many discussions concerning the Kingdom; yet, confusion and misdirection will abound. In the history of ecclesiology, much has been focused on "church history," but hardly anything on the real meaning and practice of ekklesia. Church history has been fixated on the development of various denominational churches but not on the one expression of the Body of Christ. *A clear distinction and separation are needed between churches as ministries and the Lord's ekklesia.*

Ekklesia was invented by the Greeks about 600 years before Christ. The word "ekklesia" means "called out" (*Thayer's Lexicon*). Later, Christians applied "called out" as being called out by God from the world to be His people. Christians preach that they have been "called out" from the world, so don't be "conformed" to it. However, since the Greeks invented this word, it is essential to go back to its original meaning and usage. What were the Greeks "called out" to do? Their secular usage cannot be the same as how contemporary Christians have applied that word since they practiced "ekklesia" centuries before Christ.

Ekklesia, in Greek culture, was a democratic legislative assembly. Citizens of a city-state were "called out" to have a democratic assembly to discuss, debate, and make legislation by voting. Their invention of democracy eliminated the rule of kings or emperors. It was a government of the people, by the people, and for the people. In their democracy, no one was to dominate as the sovereign, but every citizen[3] was called out and assembled to have free speech concerning various issues before placing them to a vote. There was only one ekklesia in any given city-state. All important decisions were open for debate, such as going to war, raising taxes, and building structures, with the majority making the final decision. This was how laws were enacted and decisions were made by the ekklesia.

The essential characteristics of ekklesia (democratic assembly) were the following:

1. Representation of every segment of society — The rich, the poor, the soldiers, businessmen, tradesmen, farmers, educated, uneducated, etc. Citizens of every stratum governed by that ekklesia should be included. Everyone was called out to participate.
2. Free speech — Every citizen had a right to speak their perspectives. No one was to dominate an assembly. Some may speak better than others and become gifted orators, but all had the right to speak.

When the Romans took over the Greek empire, they continued the practice of ekklesia for the community governance of their cities. There was even a secular ekklesia mentioned in Ephesus (Acts 19:32, 39). Since then, various forms of democracy continued to be the dominant system of government in the western world and beyond.

Jesus appropriated this form of Grecian government when He declared He would build His own ekklesia (democratic assembly). When Jesus said this to His disciples, no one questioned His meaning because they were all familiar with the secular ekklesia practiced in their cities. Since ekklesia is a system of government (polity), Jesus defined His ekklesia as the Kingdom of God: Those who are stones for His building have entrance into God's Kingdom. Since ekklesia was a decision-making or legislative body, Jesus gave those in His ekklesia authority to bind and loose on earth as a decision-making body.

---

3   The Greek "city states" invented "democratic assemblies" or ekklesia. A qualified "citizen" had to be 18 years or older, male, not a slave or foreigner and, in sum, Greek. Thus, though restrictive, it still constituted perhaps the first "participatory/contributory citizenry" form of polity. For more information, see David Sacks, *Encyclopedia of the Ancient Greek World*, rev. ed. (New York: Facts on File, 2005).

"Whatever you shall bind on earth shall be bound in the heavens and whatever you shall loose on earth shall be loosed in the heavens" (Matt. 16:19). God desires His Kingdom on earth. He wants the authority of the Kingdom on earth such that it is His Kingdom on earth which makes decisions on behalf of heaven. God does not want to rule in heaven as He has since eternity. He desires to transfer that authority to earth, to men (male and female) of His ekklesia.

"Your Kingdom come, Your will be done on earth as it is in heaven" (Matt. 6:10). God's problem is not in heaven where His throne is located (Psalm 11:4). His battleground is the earth. His will is that His Kingdom is on earth, the place where Satan has his Kingdom of darkness. God's purpose is that a Kingdom of His *kind* dominates and subdues the earth (Gen. 1:26-28) in order to overthrow Satan's kingdom on earth.

In a secular democracy, it is the majority of votes which become law — governed by the majority. This system, with many advantages, has also spawned corruption and unrighteousness where a slim minority of people can be swayed to affect an entire society; a collection of self-interest groups can band together to govern to the detriment of the majority, or a majority can suppress the minority. Many leading democratic countries today are full of division and hatred among those with opposing objectives and contrary perspectives.

Notwithstanding, God decided in His eternal purpose to use this very forum of kingdom government to manifest His multifaceted wisdom to Satan with all the principalities and power. "Through the ekklesia (democratic assembly), the manifold wisdom of God might now be made known to the rulers and authorities in the heavenly places. This was according to the eternal purpose" (Eph. 3:10-11).

From the invention of ekklesia until the time of the New Testament, ekklesia did not include women, slaves, foreigners, or those 18 years and under. They could not participate in speaking or voting. However, in the Lord's democratic assembly (ekklesia), both women and slaves are included (Gal. 3:28). The Lord's ekklesia/Kingdom is much more diverse than the secular ones in those days. His Kingdom includes "those from every tribe and language and people and nation" (Rev. 5:9-10).

It is in this fantastically diverse environment of God's democratic assembly as the lampstand which provides light to this dark world. While the people of the world are fighting and dividing due to differences, God's democratic assembly, including even more people who differ so greatly, are showing love, respect, and oneness among those very dissimilar from themselves. While the world seeks in vain after these qualities, the Lord's democratic assembly is brimming with love, righteousness, peace, joy, and unity in demonstration of Jesus' prayer: "That they may all be one, just as you, Father, are in me, and I in you, that they also may be in us, so that the world may believe that you have sent me" (John 17:21b ESV).

This prayer of the Lord is another way to describe the building up of His ekklesia/Kingdom. His mission was that His followers become as one as the Father and the Son. This is the light of the world which will cause the world to believe. This oneness cannot be manufactured or negotiated because it is the same unique oneness as the Father and the Son. Just as the Trinity is diverse yet one, God's democratic assembly is the enlargement, if you would, of the Trinity (God's *Kind*). It is the Kingdom of God. The manifestation of God's diverse people in oneness will convince the world of Christ's reality.

The Difference between Church and Ekklesia

Mistranslating the word "ekklesia" to "church" may be the greatest deception Satan did to attack God's eternal purpose. Due to this mistranslation, it has been utilized to segregate and divide God's people. While churches of all stripes through the centuries have preached God's word and the gospel of Jesus Christ, they also have, intentionally or unintentionally, divided God's people. The intention of this writing is not to cast a blanket condemnation on "institutional churches" or "house churches." Rather, it is to have an open consideration and discussion concerning the Kingdom of God and what is Satan's strategy in delaying its building up since the first advent of Christ. Knowing the difference between *church* and *ekklesia* (democratic assembly) is critical for this purpose.

In the sixteenth century, William Tyndale was the first translator of the Bible from Greek to English.[4] He translated the word "ekklesia" to "congregation." The Roman Church objected and demanded that the word be translated as "church." Tyndale refused to translate the word to "church," even at the cost of his life.[5] His refusal to use the word "church" in his translation was a major

---

4   John Wycliff and his associates translated from the Latin Vulgate what appears to be the entire Bible between the years AD 1384 to 1395 AD into the common Middle English vernacular—it was the first ever translation of the Bible into English.

5   William Tyndale, who was the first person to translate to English using both Hebrew and Greek, translated the Greek word *ekklesia* to "congregation." He replaced "priest" with "elder," "do penance" with "repentance," "confess" with "acknowledge," and "charity" with "love." The most offensive of his changes was his use of "congregation" for "church." The Roman Church demanded Tyndale use the word "church." His refusal to comply to this and to the antipathy of Henry VIII, eventually led to his execution. Less than one hundred years later, King James authorized another revision of his version, following Matthew's Bible, the Great Bible, and the Bishops' Bible. Out of 15 rules, rule #3 from King James: the Greek word *ekklesia* must be translated to "church." According to Donald Brake, an estimated 80 to 90 percent of the KJV heavily relied on Tyndale (Donald L. Brake, *A Visual History of the King James Bible* (Grand Rapids: Baker, 2011), 51. The KJV's usage of the word "church" rather than "congregation" cemented a pattern that has influenced nearly all English translations of the Bible.

reason the Roman Church executed Tyndale. In an effort to present him as an example; after they strangled him, they burned him at the stake.

Less than one hundred years later, King James authorized another revision of his version using 80% of Tyndale's version. However, there were 15 rules which James demanded. Rule #3 stated that the Greek word "ekklesia" had to be translated to "church." Ever since the King James translation, nearly every English translation of the New Testament followed and popularized the word "church." Now "ekklesia" is synonymous with "church" such that English-speaking Christians almost universally say, "Jesus is building His *church*," and "the *church* is the Body of Christ."

What is the meaning of the word "*church*"? The first definition, according to Marriam-Webster and most other dictionaries, is "a building for public and especially Christian worship." The etymology of the word "*church*," according to etymonline.com, is: Greek *kyriake (oikia)*, *kyriakon doma*, "the lord's (house)." "House" indicates a physical place of worship. And "lord" was not referring to Jesus, but to one of the Greek deities. In other words, it was a physical place to worship an idol.

Why was it critical to translate the word "ekklesia" to "*church*" for both the Roman church and King James? Answer: because the Roman Church owned all the churches in Europe, and King James, as the head of the Anglican Church, owned all the churches in England. Therefore, they wanted their subjects to go to church. Consider this: whoever owns the church determines what is taught in that church.

Therefore, those in authority wanted their subjects to be taught the Bible in their churches according to their perspectives. There are churches that are owned by members of the church, and they may make decisions democratically.[6] Nevertheless, the principle remains the same since those members as a group would dictate the doctrines and practices of that church.

In the last 500 years the proliferation of churches has helped spread the gospel all over the earth. Churches have generally preached the gospel of Jesus Christ and taught the Bible. However, each church has continued to teach from the perspectives of its owner. Every church is owned by a certain person, group, or ministry, and no one can freely go into a church and speak in opposition to the teachings espoused by the owner.

---

6   There are some church organizations that may operate democratically in the sense that it is owned by members of the church, and they make all major decisions by voting. For example, they will vote on who to hire as their pastor, how to spend their funds, or whether to expand or sell their church. However, once decisions are made in this group, then dissension is no longer permitted if one is to remain in this church. Therefore, this kind of church is operating as a group ministry and not the Lord's ekklesia as described in this chapter.

Therefore, churches, by design, segregate Christians according to doctrinal interpretations, music/worship styles, and the personality of ministers. These diverse emphases might be necessary just as Paul was an apostle to the Gentiles and Peter to the Jews. That may be similar reasons for ministries housed in churches catering to people of different races, languages, and other demographics. However, by making "going to church" a destination for all Christians, Satan has utilized churches to keep believers separated from each other. Churches have become factions in keeping believers from fellowshipping with each other. They are kept from the unity needed in the Kingdom of God.

> "And he gave the apostles, the prophets, the evangelists, the shepherds, and teachers, to equip the saints for the work of ministry, for building up the body of Christ, until we all attain to the unity of the faith and of the knowledge of the Son of God, to mature [perfect] manhood, to the measure of the stature of the fullness of Christ."
>
> (Eph. 4:11-13 ESV)

The leadership of churches and ministries often includes one of the "five-fold" gifted persons above. Regardless of their gifting, this Scripture confirms their commission is to equip believers through teaching Scriptures and imparting spiritual gifts. The fruit of this equipping is for all those under their tutelage to become activated and function in each of their own ministries. Then common believers directly build up the One Body of Christ in their daily lives: They arrive at the unity of the faith. Their effort is not simply to build up one of the various ministries from which they received help but to build up the whole Body of Christ, His democratic assembly.

The manifestation of building up one Body is that all believers, no matter from which church/ministry they have received equipping, come to the unity of the faith. The goal of the equipping by the gifted ministers is for common believers to arrive at unity. This is the Lord's democratic assembly (ekklesia), the Kingdom of God. Paul, in this portion of Scripture, calls this "mature manhood, the measure of the stature of the fullness of Christ."

The maturity of believers is evidenced by them being one. This corresponds with Jesus' prayer in John 17.

> "I in them and You in me, that they may be perfected [matured] into one [and] that the world may know that You have sent me, and [that] You have loved them as You have loved me."
>
> (John 17:23 DBY)

The Lord prayed a stunning and lofty prayer the night before His crucifixion: He prayed three times for His people to be as one as the Father and the Son. This oneness manifests perfection or maturity. The word "perfected" in this verse is the same as "mature" in Ephesians 4. In God's eternal plan, this oneness of His diverse people manifests as perfection or maturity. God's democratic assembly is built up when babes in Christ grow to maturity.

All ministries are to equip and supply ordinary believers who are under their care to function in the whole Body of Christ. All those equipped and functioning as common believers should be activated in each of their own ministries. This equipping enables them to arrive at the unity of the faith. All of Christ's believers subscribe to only one faith. That unique faith in Jesus Christ brings His people together in oneness.

There needs to be a radical change from "church-think," where ministers and believers only think of gathering and fellowshipping around their own ministry/church, and replace it with a focus on building the Lord's democratic assembly. If believers desire to go to the church of their choice for worship or equipping, that is not a problem. What about the rest of the time when believers are not in church? Is there a desire and seeking to fellowship with all other members in the Kingdom who may go to different churches or not at all? That is the Kingdom of God in reality, not in the divided state of churches, but in the one fellowship of the Spirit in oneness with all God's people, that is, the Lord's democratic assembly (ekklesia).

A stark contrast exists between ekklesia (democratic assembly) and church. Churches belong to a person or a group who have dominant control in that church. Whereas God's democratic assembly belongs to the Lord and all believers where the gathering is heterogeneous, while freedom of speech is one of its chief characteristics. Furthermore, no one group or person can be allowed to dominate this assembly. It is the Lord's ekklesia that is God's Kingdom. Ministries in churches should be the tools to equip and mature believers for the Kingdom.

(A complete and in-depth study of God's ekklesia is available in the book *One Ekklesia* by the same author)

BOOKS BY HENRY HON

One Ekklesia: The Vision and Practice of God's Eternal Purpose. The apostle Paul declared that God's *ekklesia* manifests His multi-faceted wisdom according to His eternal purpose (Eph. 3:10-11). His *ekklesia* was central to Jesus Christ's mission. Therefore, immediately after Peter proclaimed Jesus as "The Christ, the Son of the living God," Jesus said, "I will build My *ekklesia*," which has been mistranslated to "church" (Matt. 16:18).

Ekklesia was the forum for democracy invented by the Greeks BC 600. While secular democracies are increasing with divisions, hatred, and corruption, Jesus' *ekklesia* (democratic assembly) cultivates acceptance, forgiveness, love for one another, and unity among His people of uniqueness and diversity.

This book distinguishes between "church" as a place for ministry for preaching and teaching, and God's *ekklesia* which is also identified as the Body of Christ, God's Household, the Bride, the New Man, and the New Jerusalem. While churches have benefited many of God's people, they have also caused much division among Christians.

Jesus is calling His followers to join Him building His "democratic" Kingdom. This is not a call to start a new church or to improve churches, but for individual believers to fellowship with one another and manifest their organic unity in Christ no matter which church they attend or not attend at all. This call is in fulfillment of the Lord's prayer: "...that they may be one in us, that the world may believe..." (John 17:21).

Jesus Christ died and resurrected for His *ekklesia*. This practical oneness of diverse believers serves as a light to the world, igniting the holy fire of God, spreading uncontrollably — the next and final revival. *One Ekklesia* (336 pages)

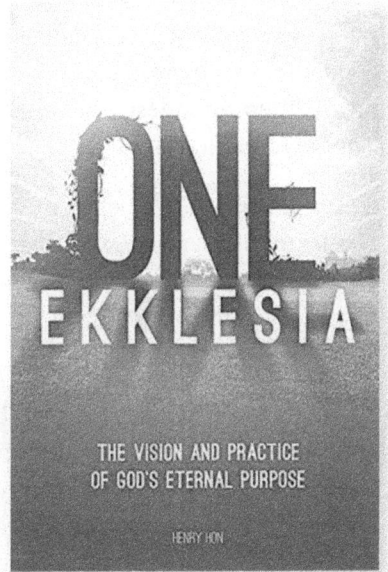

One Truth: Liberating – Nourishing – Unifying. Jesus said: The truth shall set you free and if the Son sets you free, you shall be free for real. When Jesus declared these words in John 8, the religious people of His day were first condemning an adulterous woman to death, then after Jesus saved her, they wanted to kill Jesus.

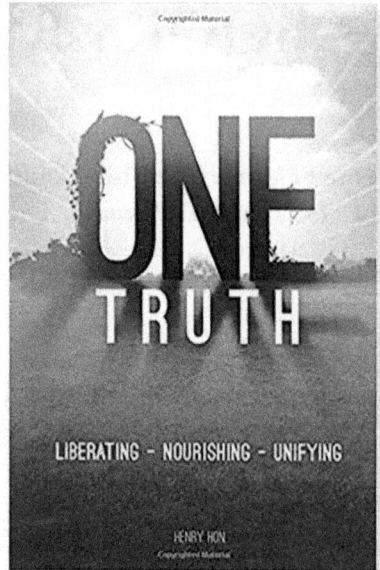

Truth liberates people from religious condemnation and its zeal that's ready to kill — if not physically then at least psychologically or spiritually.

The word "truth" in the Greek (*alethia*) means "the reality lying at the basis of appearance." People are caught up with appearances both in the secular and religious world. There is a hunger within every person for what is real. Your inner being is drained by vanity; truth is needed to nourish, sustain and energize your soul. The world is full of hostile separations. Jesus in John 17 gave the gift of truth so that the most hostile and divided people may become united. Religious dogma and ceremonial practices divide, but truth unites.

A person who has received logic and life from truth is one who can love, forgive, and express kindness to all; especially, those different or contrary to himself. Jesus answered: "I am the way, the TRUTH, and the life" (John 14:6).

Bonus: Introducing the *Completion Gospel*, which is needed today for the ending of the age. Most of the gospel heard by people today is basically only half of it. The entire gospel needs to be preached! *ONE TRUTH*. (278 pages)

One Life & Glory: Miraculously Normal Living and Service. Both Christians and non-Christians like to witness the supernatural, miraculous actions taken by God. Certainly, God can do miracles to heal your loved ones from terminal diseases or to solve all your financial worries with a lottery winning. However, God's desire with humanity is not to be their "Santa Claus"; His desire and purpose is wonderful beyond imagination: He wants to be "miraculously normal" in humanity. Not just hit and miss miraculous events here and there, but miraculous every day, such that it is normal and ordinary.

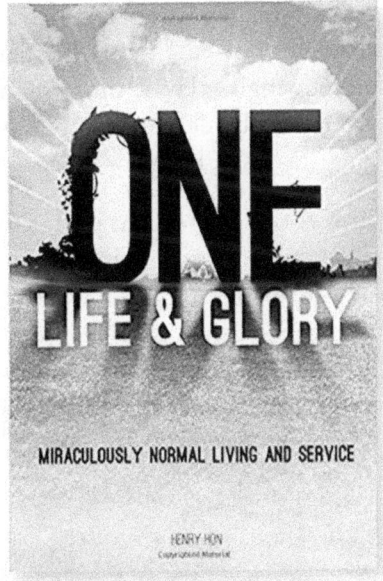

This is God Himself being the source, empowering humanity to live by His divine-eternal life through faith in Jesus Christ. Being miraculously normal means: it will be indistinguishable whether it is you or God who is loving, caring, forgiving, enduring, and living in this present world. Moreover, services rendered to both God and humanity can likewise be miraculously normal.

Ordinary words can be spoken; yet, they can give eternal life to the hearer. Through normal interactions peace can be made between people previously divided and hostile with one another; they are brought into fellowship. This book, *One in Life and Glory*, is the third in this series forming a Trilogy together with: *One Ekklesia* and *One Truth*. This Trilogy of *ONE* expounds on the Lord's prayer in John 17 for all His people to become one — as one as the Father and the Son are one. In His prayer, He gave three gifts to accomplish the oneness of His people: eternal life, truth (the "logos" or His Word) and His glory. When previously divided, even hostile people, can become one in this present conflicting and confusing age; then the people of the world will believe "the Father sent the Son" — our Lord Jesus Christ. *One Life & Glory* (332 pages)

Galatians: Uniting Divided People examines how and why Christians have unknowingly played into Satan's plan of division by de-emphasizing and even ignoring Jesus' heart for unity.

This is the gospel that unites us: Jesus died on the cross for the forgiveness of sins to justify His followers by faith. However, most overlook that Jesus died not only for our individual sins but also "to gather into one the children of God who are scattered abroad" (John 11:52, ESV).

This book exposes Satan's craftiness in using the gifts of God and laws in Scriptures to create divergent brands of churches and groups. Christians have unwittingly, distorted the gospel resulting in more and more divisions.

Jesus prayed that our unity would look like the Trinity: diverse yet one (John 17:22, 23, ESV). This is good news! Christians can have opposing perspectives and experiences but still love, respect, serve, and forgive one another, as one.

When followers of Jesus Christ are more divided than the secular world, Galatians provides the solution. God reveals this reality as a light: "There is neither Jew nor Greek, there is neither slave nor free, there is no male and female, for you are all one in Christ Jesus" (Gal. 3:28). **Galatians: Uniting Divided People** (95 pages)

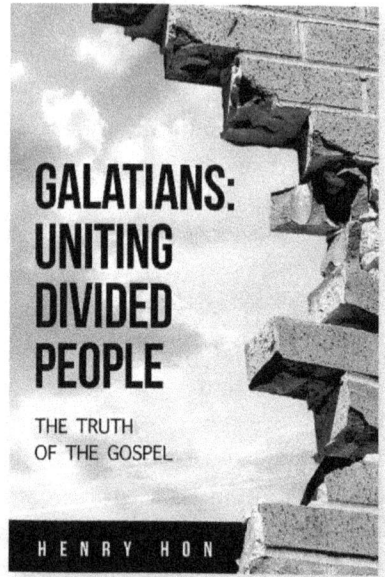

God's Kind: The Glory and Triumph of God's Kingdom. "God's Kind" here does not mean "God is kind," even though He certainly is. Rather, it refers to God's species or children. Using "God's Kind" to expound on the Kingdom of God is new and bold. The hope is to jolt readers to think outside the "Kingdom of God box," which has been rigidly constructed within the various perspectives of major theological schools and has continued to divide Christians.

Satan's attack on God's *kind* is focused on this truism spoken by Jesus: "Every kingdom divided against itself is laid waste, and a divided household falls" (Luke 11:17b ESV). Satan manipulates immature believers to increase division in God's Kingdom. Consequently, divided believers are made weak, sickly, poor, and ineffectual.

This comprehensive study of God's Kingdom from Genesis to Revelation exposes Satan's tactics of dividing God's children and should motivate them to grow to maturity. God's Kingdom is not a "theocracy," as most would assume. Rather, His desire is for a diverse democratic Kingdom where each of His *kind* can be liberated as distinct individuals. Yet, they love one another in fellowship, expressing the oneness of the Trinity.

Love and oneness express the divine life (DNA) within God's *kind* — God's Kingdom. Seek first His Kingdom, and He will richly provide all things needed for the present life and a rich entrance into the coming Kingdom of God in glory. Immature believers may find themselves unfavorably judged at the Judgment Seat of Christ. Instead of reigning with Christ in the Millennial Kingdom, those who stay babes may need another period to grow before the Eternal Kingdom.

Being a child of God is an awesome privilege; nevertheless, each person is responsible for building God's Kingdom. Bringing God's Kingdom to earth in the present age is an abundant blessing of life, grace, and purpose. God's *kind* will triumph over Satan's kingdom and ultimately give glory to God. **GOD'S KIND** (250 pages)

These books and their e-book compliments, as well as AUDIO on these books can be found @ www.onebody.life and on Amazon.com.

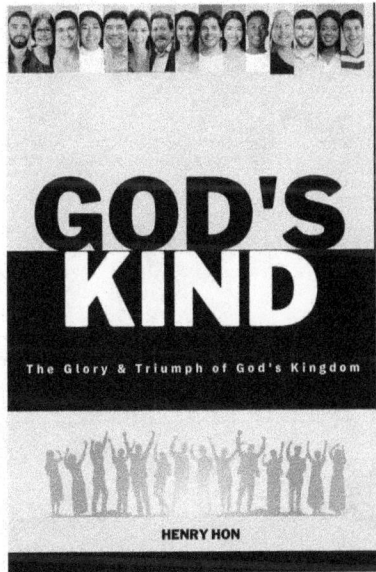

www.ingramcontent.com/pod-product-compliance
Lightning Source LLC
Chambersburg PA
CBHW020438030426
42337CB00014B/1308